# The Government of
# England under Elizabeth

*By Conyers Read*

PUBLISHED FOR

THE FOLGER SHAKESPEARE LIBRARY

Cornell University Press

ITHACA, NEW YORK

CORNELL UNIVERSITY PRESS

*First published 1960*

*Second printing 1964*

PRINTED IN THE UNITED STATES OF AMERICA

SOME five years after Elizabeth's accession to the throne Sir Thomas Smith wrote the first account of her government. Sir Thomas was a man of many parts, one of the distinguished Greek scholars of his time, Regius professor of civil law at Cambridge under Henry VIII, Principal Secretary to Henry's son Edward, Member of Parliament, Privy Councillor, Principal Secretary under Elizabeth. He had besides a facile pen. No man in England was better qualified to write of her government. His discourse, *De republica Anglorum,* was not published until 1583, six years after his death, but it ran through five editions before the end of the reign.

Smith adds very little to our knowledge of the subject. The value of his discourse is its revelation of how the government appeared to a contemporary.

The earlier chapters of Smith's book reflected his classical background and consisted of a classification of different types of government after the pattern of Aristotle's *Politics.* Like Aristotle, he singled out three main types, monarchy, aristocracy, democracy, and went on to say that perfect examples of any one type were rare. Most commonwealths were a mixture. Although he did not precisely say so, he evidently regarded the Elizabethan government as a mixture of monarchial and aristocratic elements.

His approach to the government was by a definition of the people governed. "We in England," he wrote, "divide our men commonly into five sorts: gentlemen, citizens, yeomen, artificers and laborers."

The first three sorts are those which one way or another participate in the government. The fourth group Smith defined more particularly as day laborers, poor husbandmen—those who had no free land—and all artificers not yeomen or citizens. "These," he wrote, "have no voice nor authority in our commonwealth and no account is made of them but only to be ruled, not to rule others." And yet, he went on to say that at the local level men of this poorer sort were sometimes utilized for jury duty, or as churchwardens and constables.

Smith, in short, recognized and accepted a society of classes. He accepted no doubt what was known as the great chain of being, the social implications of which were well set forth in the 1547 book of homilies as follows:

Every degree of people in their vocation, calling, and office hath appointed to them their duty and order. Some are in high degree, some in low; some kings and princes, some inferiors and subjects; priests and laymen, masters and servants, fathers and children, husbands and wives, rich and poor and every one have need of other so that in all things is to be lauded and praised the goodly order of God without the which no house, no city, no commonwealth, can continue and endure.

The classic expression of this pattern of society is the speech which Shakespeare put into Ulysses' mouth in *Troilus and Cressida*, "Take but degree away, untune that string, and hark what discord follows."

The important fact is the general endorsement and justification of political and social inequality. On the political side it was the negation of the democratic principle. Democratic rule was indeed generally discredited everywhere in the sixteenth century, in all governments and all creeds, and those who advocated it were regarded very much as we in the West today regard Communists; and everywhere democratic advocates were persecuted. Sir Thomas in one place insisted that the classes should be marked by their attire. "A gentleman," he wrote, "must go like a gentleman, a yeoman like a yeoman, a rascal like a rascal." By rascal he meant not a bad fellow but a base fellow. This explains in part the persistent efforts of the government to control apparel.

In the sixteenth century the social reformers, by and large, preached not equality but the due recognition by each class of its duties and responsibilities. This of course did not mean that the various classes were enclosed in watertight compartments. The class system was not breaking down, but there was a steady recruitment of the upper classes from the lower classes. The yeoman might, and often did, gather together enough property to enter the ranks of the gentry. What was more important, prosperous townsmen, aspiring to be gentry, were buying their way into the countryside. Sir Thomas pointed out: "As for gentlemen, they be made good cheap in England. For whosoever studieth the laws of the realm, who studieth in the universities, who professeth liberal sciences, and, to be short, who can live idly and without manual labor, and will bear the port, charge, and countenance of a gentleman, he shall be called Master . . . and shall be taken for a gentleman . . . and (if need be) a king of Heralds shall also give him for money arms newly made and invented." It was merely a matter of money or its equivalent; even the pedigree was a matter of money.

The same thing was true in the further ascent from the gentry to the nobility. Elizabeth herself was very chary about creating peers, but most of the great noblemen in her reign were recent upstarts. Of sixty-two peers in 1560, thirty-seven held titles conferred since the accession of her father. The Dudleys, the Sidneys, the Russells, the Wriothesleys, the Herberts, the Cecils, all belonged in that category. The Wars of the Roses had pretty well wiped out the old nobility. Their titles perhaps survived but often had been transferred to new men. If the bottles were old, the wine was new.

But there was a flow from class to class both ways. If some were climbing up, others were slipping down. The law of primogeniture which controlled the descent of the title and the real property, while providing for the first-born, made no provision at all for the younger son, who had more or less to shift for himself. Without real estate, the current coin of wealth and social prestige, he tended to go downwards, from nobility to gentry, from gentry to yeomanry, from yeomanry to something below. The result was a certain blurring of class levels, accentuated by a good deal of intermarriage. There was nothing hard and fast about English class lines, as there was for example in France under the old régime.

The process of change within the social pattern was quickened by the wholesale confiscation of church lands associated with the break from Rome. This land came into the real-estate market and a considerable part of it was purchased by the nouveaux riches who had made their fortunes in the city or in public office. Land, after all, in the days before stocks and bonds, provided one of the few opportunities for profitable investment. The purchasers brought to the countryside the attitudes and impulses of the market place, with little of the traditional and sentimental obligations recognized by the country gentlemen of the old school. For these newcomers, agriculture was not a way of life; it was a source of profit. They expected a yield upon their investments and presently discovered that rents might be raised and arable land enclosed and turned into pasture land to advantage. The social reformers of the time were constantly venting their spleen upon the encloser and the rack-renter. As Sir Thomas More put it, sheep were eating up men. The change was perhaps inevitable, but the death throes of a feudal, self-sustaining economy and the rise of a capitalist, profit-making economy were hard on the little man and brought about a great deal of distress and unrest. The sporadic riots which plagued the Elizabethan justices of the peace in almost every county in England were the fruits of this unrest; so was the marked increase in unemployment. One of the fears which constantly beset William Cecil in his forty-odd years of service as Elizabeth's chief counselor was that any foreign invader would find a great deal of domestic discontent to support him.

Queen Elizabeth at the age of twenty-five, without any overt opposition, ascended the English throne in November, 1558. She certainly had the best claim to it by inheritance, though her father, Henry VIII, repudiated his marriage to her mother and she had been declared a bastard by act of Parliament. The act still stood on the statute book at her accession, though Parliament had subsequently given to Henry the right to determine the succession, and Henry had named Elizabeth to succeed her half-sister Mary. There were those who maintained that Henry's will was a forgery. There were even those who asserted that Elizabeth's father was not Henry but her mother's paramour. But England at large accepted Elizabeth with enthusiasm.

She was unmarried, and until she did marry and have children she was the last of the direct Tudor line. Henry's will provided that, in default of offspring to Elizabeth, the succession should pass to the descendents of his younger sister Mary, the so-called Suffolk line, though actually the descendents of Henry's older sister Margaret, the so-called Stuart line, had the prior claim. There were other claimants as well.

At the time of Elizabeth's accession, the Suffolk line was represented by Catherine Grey, sister of the unfortunate Lady Jane Grey; the Stuart line by Mary Stuart, married to the Dauphin of France, already Queen of Scotland and presently to be Queen of France. English Protestants favored the Suffolk line, English Catholics the Stuart line. Elizabeth herself was noncommital. To the very end she remained noncommital.

The preferred solution of course was that she should marry and bear children. Until she was past childbearing age she was under constant pressure to marry, or if not to marry, to designate her successor. Parliament pressed her hard, particularly in the first decade of her reign, fearing that if she died, as she came near dying in 1562, the throne would pass to the Catholic Mary and the whole battle for the faith would have to be fought all over again. But neither Parliament nor the constant urgings of Lord Burghley, her most trusted counselor, prevailed. Elizabeth died unmarried. Indeed, she made a virtue of her spinsterhood. During the last twenty years of her reign, when everybody had abandoned hope of her marriage, they glorified her as the Virgin Queen.

She was without doubt the chief figure in her government, under God and under the law. And she could and did dispense with the application of the law in particular cases. The export trade of unfinished cloth, for example, was prohibited by law, and yet, by special license from the Crown, the export of unfinished cloth was the most important commodity in the English export trade. She could by proclamation come near to making the law, though it does not appear that she ever used the proclamation that way. She could and did assume the right to initiate legislation, though she did not always succeed in imposing her will upon the lawmaking body. She could exercise an absolute veto on laws passed by both Houses of Parliament. She had complete control over appointments to all offices under the Crown, including the judges of all the courts, even including the justices of the peace, and could at her pleasure dismiss any one of them. In fact, she delegated a considerable amount of patronage. In the administration of her finances, for example, Lord Burghley, her Lord Treasurer, appointed virtually all the officials having to do with the royal revenues, except those at the highest level, and he could generally influence the Queen to accept his choice in those.

In foreign affairs she was supreme and could make war or peace at her will. In practice she never declared war without the advice of her Council, though she often sought to make peace when her Councillors opposed it. The entire personnel in foreign affairs she herself appointed. It is to be observed however that throughout her reign she had a resident ambassador in only one country, France, though she generally had a representative in Scotland and, after 1584, in the Dutch Low Countries. In Spain she had no resident ambassador after Dr. John Man's recall in 1567. She did however finance a secret intelligence service overseas organized by her Principal Secretaries, first by William Cecil, later by Walsingham, and ultimately by Robert Cecil; and on occasion she talked in person with the agents themselves.

Financially she enjoyed a considerable revenue from the rentals of Crown lands and from feudal dues. She also received the customary grant of the customs revenue for life at the beginning of her reign. The import and export duties were for the most part ad valorem duties, the percentage fixed by statute, but the basis for calculation was provided by a book of rates prepared by royal officials. By the simple expedient of increasing the prices in the book of rates she could, within reason, automatically increase the customs revenues. At times she farmed out customs revenues in particular ports or on particular commodities to private individuals. Robert, Earl of Essex, for example, had the farm of the import duties on sweet wines and made a handsome thing of it. Elizabeth's refusal to renew the grant in 1601 was the turning point of his fate.

All these independent sources of revenue taken together were inadequate to meet the ordinary expenses of government. What was short had to be made up by taxes levied by Parliament on the laity and by Convocation on the clergy. Elizabeth did not like to ask her people for money and on occasion liquidated some of the Crown lands rather than call on Parliament for taxes. Nevertheless, as time went on, and particularly after the outburst of war in 1585, she had to depend more and more on Parliamentary grants. And the burden of taxation grew steadily heavier upon her subjects.

Elizabeth's chief instrument of administration was the Privy Council, all appointed by herself. Their numbers varied at different times, never exceeding twenty. Some who were nominally of the Council rarely attended. And the active members of the Council were less than a dozen. But if we may judge from the records kept of their proceedings, they were more concerned as a body with the details of administration than with the formulation of policy. In really important matters there was an inner circle upon which Elizabeth chiefly depended. Foremost among these was William Cecil, Principal Secretary during the first fourteen years of her reign, Lord Burghley and Lord High Treasurer for the next twenty-eight years. Whatever his title, he was her chief counselor. She almost never reached an important decision without consulting him. Even so she was always the dominating figure and he always the obedient servant. Next to him in point of influence probably was Robert Dudley, Earl of Leicester, who had, and retained till the end of his days, a unique hold upon the Queen's affections. He was far inferior to Cecil in ability, in diligence, and in disinterested love of country. During the first decade of the reign Leicester's one consuming objective was to marry Elizabeth. After twenty years he finally abandoned hope and took another wife. Yet he never lost his place in her regard. According to the historian William Camden, within a month of Leicester's death in August, 1588, Elizabeth seriously contemplated appointing him to be Lieutenant General of the kingdom. Leicester appealed to the woman in Elizabeth, Cecil to the Queen. Apart from the Queen's marriage, which Leicester always aimed to prevent and Cecil to promote, they were not widely at variance in matters of policy, except that Leicester subordinated policy to personal interest, and Cecil's principal objective was always the welfare of Queen and country.

The other Councillors who belonged to the inner ring were Nicholas Bacon, the Lord Keeper in the first decade; Sir Francis Walsingham, who succeeded Cecil as Principal Secretary; and Sir Christopher Hatton in the second and third decades; Robert, Earl of Essex, and Robert Cecil in the fourth decade. Hatton and Essex belonged among the Queen's favorites, but were both men of marked ability. Hatton became first the eloquent spokesman of the Queen in the House of Commons and later her Lord Chancellor. Essex was an able soldier and a clever politician, but was "of a nature not be ruled" and finally ended a brilliant career at the block.

It is to be noted that during Elizabeth's reign only one ecclesiastic was a member of the Privy Council, and that the important members were all commoners, or else, like Leicester and Burghley, peers of her own creation.

It has been said that Elizabeth, like her father, deliberately nourished factions in her Privy Council on the principle of divide and rule. Certainly factions developed—in the first decade the Cecilians vs. the Leicesterians, in the last decade the Cecilians vs. Essex. In the second and third decades, when the Puritans were strong in the Council, the division expressed itself chiefly in foreign policy, the Puritans aiming to subordinate national considerations to religious ones, the *politiques* aiming to subordinate religious to national interests. Leicester was the titular head of the Puritans, Burghley of the *politiques*. But the driving spirit in the Puritan faction was Francis Walsingham. After Leicester's death in 1588 and Walsingham's in 1590, the Puritan faction faded away and was in a sense displaced by a war party led by Essex and a peace party led by the Cecils, father and son. But it is easy to overemphasize these lines of cleavage. There was a great deal of the Puritan in Burghley, and when the wars came he was as stout a supporter of military and naval operations as anyone was.

The Privy Councillors were not all of one type, but those upon whom Elizabeth chiefly depended, with the exception of Leicester and Essex, were able and patriotic public servants. They were always subordinate to their mistress. The two who tried to coerce her, Norfolk halfheartedly, Essex belligerently, lost their heads—figuratively and literally lost their heads.

Generally speaking, those in the Queen's service were inadequately paid. But they were allowed to exploit their official positions to increase their income, by fees, by perquisites, by the sale of offices under their control, and by lucrative concessions of various sorts. Indeed, public officials from top to bottom sustained themselves by the practice of what we should call graft. Even Cecil himself, otherwise a model of integrity, grew rich from the sale of wardships under his control as Master of the Court of Wards. Elizabeth in this respect was penny-wise and pound-foolish. What she gave away was worth considerably more than what it would have cost her to provide adequate compensation for her servants. Her armies were shot through with corruption. Fortunately her navy was in honest and competent hands.

Next to herself, the most important part of Elizabeth's government was her Parliament, composed of two houses, the House of Lords and the House of Commons.

The Lords were made up of the hereditary lay peers and the spiritual peers, that is, the two archbishops and the twenty-odd bishops of the Anglican church. The lay peers outnumbered the spiritual peers two to one. Altogether there were some ninety members of the Upper House. The spiritual peers were appointed by the Queen and could be discharged by the Queen. On more than one occasion she threatened to "unfrock" them. Archbishop Grindal was in fact deprived of his office because he was too favorably inclined towards the Puritans. As for the lay peers, they might not be discharged but they might be outnumbered. The Queen might create as many new ones as she pleased. In point of fact she created very few new peers. They were not necessary to strengthen her position in the Lords. On one occasion when she proposed new creations, she discovered that her candidates were not disposed to accept title unless they were provided with estates to sustain it, and that the thrifty Queen was not willing to supply. Burghley himself refused promotion from a barony to an earldom on those grounds.

The Lords were indeed very tractable to the royal wishes. Their presiding officer was the Keeper of the Great Seal, or his equivalent, the Lord Chancellor. During the first decade of the reign Nicholas Bacon occupied that office. But after Cecil was raised to the peerage in 1571 he appears to have looked after the Queen's interests in the Upper House until he died twenty-seven years later. The Lords were called to the meeting of Parliament by writs directed to each one individually. If they were unable to attend, they might give their proxies to some other peer, a privilege denied to the members of the Lower House.

Bills might originate in either house, though it was generally recognized that money bills (i.e., those levying taxes) should originate in the Commons. On one occasion, when Burghley thought the taxes offered by the Lower House were inadequate to meet the royal needs and proposed to introduce a bill in the Lords supplying more, he had to accept rebuke from the Commons.

The more important and far more independent house was the House of Commons. It was elected. When the Parliament was summoned, royal writs went down to the sheriff of each county directing him to arrange for elections in the various constituencies. There were two types of constituency—first the counties, second the boroughs. The English counties elected two members each to represent them in the Commons; the boroughs generally sent two members. Boroughs were simply urban communities within the counties which had, one way or another, acquired the right to separate representation in the House of Commons. The Crown might create new boroughs at pleasure. It would have been an obvious way to strengthen the government position in the Lower House. Elizabeth indeed created or restored thirty-one boroughs, adding sixty-two members to the Commons. But there is no evidence that this action was taken to pack Parliament. The increase seems to have been due rather to local pressures than to government interest. At the end of the reign the House of Commons numbered 462.

County elections were held in the County Court, which met once a month and was made up of those freeholders within the county who held freehold land to the annual rental value of forty shillings. Generally the value of land was expressed in terms of annual rental. Since the usual price for land bought and sold was designated as twenty years' purchase, i.e., twenty times the annual rental, the county voter had to hold land by freehold tenure worth at least £40. This debarred smaller freeholders; it also debarred those whose land was held by some other tenure or was leased or rented.

Within boroughs the right of franchise varied. In the great majority of cases it seems to have been limited to a small oligarchy which controlled the town government. In all except a few cases the voters in the town were a small minority of its inhabitants.

The great majority of Englishmen had nothing to say about the election of M.P.'s. Nevertheless, as Sir Thomas Smith declared, "The consent of Parliament was taken to be every man's consent."

The borough members made up something like four-fifths of the House of Commons. It might have been presumed that urban interests would have dominated the assembly. But there is no evidence in the debates as recorded or in the ensuing legislation of any conflict of urban and rural interests. The reason for this is not far to seek. The boroughs preferred to be represented by the gentry. In only a few of the larger cities, in London, for example, were they represented by citizens. The consequence was that very much the same type of man sat for the county and for the borough within the county. Sometimes the poorer boroughs were moved by pecuniary considerations. They had to pay wages to their member, two shillings a day. But even the more important boroughs wanted a patron, a friend in high places, and the ambitious country gentlemen wanted an opportunity to spend some time in London, to visit the Court, perhaps even to kiss the hand of the Queen. The lawyers were particularly eager to sit, since Parliament usually met in term time and gave them an opportunity to pursue their legal business. The county seat offered them greater prestige, but failing a county the gentleman would settle for a borough. Contested elections in both county and borough reveal the fact that the issues at stake were not primarily political or even religious, but as to whether a Cecil or an Essex would win the place. Instead of one gentleman to four townsmen, Elizabeth's later Parliaments contained four gentlemen to every townsman.

Elizabeth generally summoned Parliament because she needed money. Altogether, in a reign of forty-four years, she called ten Parliaments, but the Parliament of 1563 sat again after a long prorogation in 1567, and the Parliament of 1572 sat again in 1576 and again in 1581. So there were really thirteen Parliaments. The largest interval between Parliaments was four years. Parliament was not regarded as part of the ordinary machinery of government. In only two cases—her first Parliament in 1559 to establish her religious settlement and her sixth Parliament in 1586 to deal with Mary Queen of Scots—can it be said that the purpose of calling them was not primarily fiscal. Cecil on more than one occasion when war was in question advised that Parliament should be consulted, but Elizabeth would not have it so.

She tried to manage her Parliaments, and always saw to it

12

that some of her Privy Councillors were present. During the first decade of her reign William Cecil was her spokesman in the Commons, and when he was elevated to the peerage in 1571 he occupied the same position in the Lords. Sir Christopher Hatton was elected to the Commons and he acted as spokesman for the Queen until his appointment to be Lord Chancellor in 1587. During the last decade of her reign Robert Cecil served in that position. All three of them were competent speakers—Hatton particularly so. It was part of their business also to maintain harmony between Crown and Commons. In this particular they were not altogether successful. Elizabeth did not get on well with her Parliaments. They were quite prepared to grant her the taxes she asked for, but they wanted things from her in return. They wanted a definite commitment from her on her marriage and on the succession in case her marriage should be fruitless. Above all they wanted reforms in the established church—in its vestments, its ritual, and its government. All of these demands she refused to entertain, on the grounds that they were her business, not theirs.

Parliamentary money grants took two forms, both of them inherited from earlier times. The first was the so-called fifteenth and tenth, which had a long history; the other was the subsidy. The fifteenth and tenth, originally a tax on movables, became a fixed amount in the fourteenth century, attached to lands rather than to movables and apportioned among the counties. There was no reassessment, each county paid what it had paid before. It amounted in the sixteenth century to £32,000. The subsidy, first introduced in Henry VIII's reign, attempted to tax income from wages and rents as well as movables. It too came to a fixed sum distributed among the counties. By the end of Elizabeth's reign it produced about £80,000. Action by Parliament in the matter was always in terms of these units. Grants were for fifteenths and tenths or a multiple of them and for subsidies or a multiple of them. In 1593, for example, Parliament granted six fifteenths and tenths and three subsidies. Usually payments were made in installments over a period of two or three years. During the last decade of Elizabeth's reign the average taxpayer paid some one of these installments annually.

The objection to this form of tax was that it laid the burden where it had been and made little or no attempt to relate the burden to the distribution of wealth. In the case of the fifteenth and tenth the burden was distributed as it had been in 1334. No reassessment was made. The burden was distributed by local assessors, appointed by the local M.P.'s, generally on the basis of land holdings, not personalty. All taxes in England tended to fall upon the land, because a man's land could not be concealed; his movable property could.

In the case of the subsidy, the commissioners in charge of collection were appointed by the Crown, though the actual assessing was by local committees appointed by the commissioners. A taxpayer's rating was recorded in what was known as a subsidy book. If his name appeared in that book he became "a subsidy man." It exposed him to all sorts of other local tax burdens; poor relief, musters, ship money, what not. So Elizabethans tried to keep their names out of the subsidy book or to keep their ratings as low as might be. The influential were outrageously under assessed, and the burden, both of the fifteenth and tenth and of the subsidy, fell disproportionately upon the less well to do. In 1593 Burghley observed that some of the richest landowners in England were not taxed above £80 in land, and in London, "where was the greatest part of the riches of the realm," none above £200 in goods, and but eight above £100.

He pointed out that one subsidy, honestly assessed, would yield as much as three subsidies as currently collected. But nothing effective was done about it. Even with the inequalities, the tax burden upon the English was far lighter than it was elsewhere. There were no excises, no profits taxes unless those profits found expression in increased receipts from rentals, in increased stocks of merchandise, or in increased luxuries in living. It is interesting to note that the rate of tax on jewelry in the subsidy bill of 1593 was higher than on other forms of property. But one doubts whether much or any of it found its way into the subsidy book.

Parliament was commonly referred to in the sixteenth century as the High Court, but such judicial functions as it actually exercised in that century were attached to the Lords, who occasionally heard appeals on writs of error from lower courts. It was primarily a lawmaking body, with no constitutional limit upon its legislative power except the royal veto.

In practice the superior courts in England were the Court of Queen's Bench, which heard criminal pleas, otherwise called pleas of the Crown; the Court of Common Pleas, which heard pleas on matters civil; the Court of Exchequer which dealt with cases arising out of the royal revenues; and the Court of Chancery, which dealt with cases in equity. All of these Courts met in Westminster Hall.

Twice a year between law terms, during Lent and midsummer, when the Queen's Bench and Common Pleas were not in session, the judges divided into couples and each couple went on circuit to the six different circuits into which England was divided. They held court for all pleas in each of the counties within their circuit, usually sitting from one to three days, at the county seat. The Sheriff of the county attended to local arrangements, submitted a panel of jurors, and had the defendants and the plaintiffs involved at hand. He was also expected to entertain the visiting judges. These local sessions were originally designed to maintain uniformity in the common law administration at Westminster and in the counties, and to curb local bias and prejudice. Like all the Elizabethan courts, their function was not confined to matters judicial. The justices on assize conveyed the royal purposes and the royal wishes to the county at large and kept the Crown informed of local conditions, local attitudes, local desires. They were indeed the vital connecting link between the Queen and her counties.

There were besides other courts established by the Tudor monarchs to try cases with which the royal courts for one reason or another appeared incompetent to deal. The most significant of these was the Court of Star Chamber, made up of the Queen's Privy Council with the Chief Justices of the Queen's Bench and the Common Pleas. Its procedure followed rather the pattern of the Roman civil law than of the common law. Testimony from witnesses was taken in writing. There was no jury. Star Chamber, named for the room in Westminster Hall where it sat, had been organized by Henry VII to deal with civil disorders. It was used for many other purposes, largely for dealing with disobedience to royal commands. On one occasion it tried William Davison, the Queen's Secretary, for indiscretion in the interpretation of royal orders. It dealt with forgery, slander, libel. Strangely enough, it became for a time the tribunal to which disputed elections for the House of Commons were referred.

It was regarded askance by the common lawyers but was not unpopular with the rank and file of the people, who looked to it for protection against powerful nobles in the country whom local juries did not dare find guilty. Later, under the Stuarts, when the issue was definitely joined between the Crown and Parliament, it was violently attacked, and like all the other so-called prerogative courts it was swept away in the Great Rebellion. Other prerogative courts were the Court of Requests, set up for dealing with poor men's cases, and the Court of Wards, which administered the royal wards of the Crown and contributed not a little to the royal revenues, to say nothing of the perquisites to its officials. Under Elizabeth, the Mastership of the Wards was regarded as the choicest plum in the gift of the Crown. Lord Burghley held that position during most of Elizabeth's reign and made a modest fortune out of it.

It was through the judiciary that the Queen maintained her contact with local government. And it was the local justices of the peace into whose hands by little and little the control of local government passed.

The justices were named by the Lord Chancellor in a Commission of the Peace which was issued at irregular intervals. Their term of office was not defined and in the majority of cases they served for life. But new names could be added and old ones dropped by the issue of a new Commission. Elizabeth herself kept a close eye upon the J.P.'s and revised the list from time to time. Their number varied from twenty to sixty in each county. In 1589 there were 1,738 all told.

The law provided that J.P.'s should have at least £20 income from lands. They were in fact of the gentry, including some noblemen, and were of course residents of the county in which they sat. This gave the county a comfortable sense of being ruled by one of their own and not by a "foreigner," an imposed outsider. The J.P.'s taken as a whole were in fact the natural leaders of the country. Unlike the French noblesse, they lived in the countryside which they governed and understood it, though more than once the Queen had to admonish them for flocking to London and the Court and to send them home. They were from the same class, by and large they were the same men, who sat in the House of Commons. It might almost be said that they made the law at Westminster, interpreted it, and enforced it in the county. Consequently, statute law became sometimes rather a register of good resolutions than an effective order, particularly if the enforcement of it ran counter to the interests of the gentry class. What they said in Westminster they could more or less gainsay in the counties. Their local autonomy was in fact very considerable.

Generally speaking, the office of justice of the peace was held by the great county families. The listing of them was a sort of local social register. Although the office was not hereditary, it often passed on from father to son. We have here indeed a sort of revived feudalism in which the local magistrate was the lord of the manor, supported by the traditional loyalties of the countryside. Very often he held the right of advowson to the village church; that is to say, he nominated the rector. As legislator in the Commons, he placed in his own hands the fixing of wages, the maintenance of the roads, and the care of the poor, and he applied all these in his own interest. As Kenneth Pickthorn observes in *Early Tudor Government: Henry VII* (Cambridge, Eng., 1934), what the gentry wanted done, the Crown could get done very easily; what they did not mind being done, it could get easily enough. What would happen if the Crown should want something which that class was determined should not be done, was a question still to be settled, even still to be raised.

The justice could act as magistrate, alone or with another, but his more extended powers were expressed in the assembly of the justices of the county, four times a year, in Quarter Sessions. For that meeting, as for the semiannual courts of the judge of assize, the Sheriff provided a panel for a grand jury of presentment and for trial juries, and saw to it that plaintiffs and defendants were on hand. It was a considerable company and came as near to a county assembly as England was to come. In this respect it had displaced the County Court, which had lost most of its significance and become little more than a gathering of voters for county members to Parliament. William Lambarde, the Kentish antiquary, in charging the grand jury at Kent Quarter Sessions, more than once pointed out with pride that the law was locally applied and enforced not by "foreign" officials but by kinsfolk and neighbors. They determined in a local grand jury who should be tried and by a local petty jury who were innocent and who were guilty. The trouble was, as Lambarde insisted, that, whether for fear or favor, the grand jury did not present and the trial jury would not condemn. That, he thought, was the reason why prerogative courts like Star Chamber were springing up and the liberties of Englishmen were by little and little diminished.

In the Commission of the Peace distinction was made between the ordinary judges and those specifically designated whose presence was essential for certain decisions. These special ones came to be known as "of the quorum." At the outset they were men learned in the law and served to prevent unlearned colleagues from acting counter to the law. The commission also provided for a *custos rotulorum*, keeper of the county records. He appointed the Clerk of the Peace and was, if any one was, the President Justice. The office had considerable local prestige and later was generally, though not always, conferred upon the Lord Lieutenant when that office was created.

The J.P., the Clerk of the Peace and even Shakespeare's "coram" and "custalorum" were often the butt of the dramatists. Too often they knew no law, and there was a flourishing book business in guides for the justices in the sixteenth and seventeenth centuries. But what they lacked in law, which could generally be supplied by their clerks, they more than made up by their acquaintance with the countryside. Their administrative duties were probably more important than their judicial duties, and the Crown looked largely to them in all local matters from the fixing of wages to the collection of taxes and the levy of troops.

The Sheriff was the old leader of Crown officials in the county and he still continued to function as the titular head of the county. His official duties were in part fiscal, in part judicial, in large measure social. He was in general responsible for the police of the county, the keeping of the jails, the execution of capital punishment. He held office for one year only and was annually selected by the Queen herself from a list of eligibles, in the ceremony known as "the pricking of the sheriffs." It was generally held that he should have some military experience, though when the wars came he was nudged aside and the military aspects of the county passed into the hands of the Lord Lieutenant and his deputies.

The Lord Lieutenant was usually a nobleman, very often a Privy Councillor. Quite frequently two or three counties were assigned to one Lord Lieutenant. And there were counties which had none. Generally speaking, the imminence of war quickened the royal interest in the office. That was so in 1569; it was so in 1588. The office conferred great social prestige. Burghley himself made a great point of it and felt abused when the Lord Lieutenantship of a county in which he had an interest went to someone else. He was indeed Lord Lieutenant of three counties: Lincolnshire, Herts, and Essex.

Being no soldier, Burghley functioned through Deputy Lieutenants. So did most of the others, generally appointing Deputies from the local gentry. It was felt that half-trained troops would serve better under officers selected from the natural leaders of their own counties. Actually there was an acute shortage of seasoned officers. What few there were with actual battle experience were in Ireland and the Low Countries. But they were fighting England's battles in both places and could not be too heavily drawn upon.

The army, such as it was, was based upon the musters of all the able-bodied men (sixteen to sixty) in the kingdom. Some part of them received a little training and were alluded to as the trained bands. Probably the most intensive effort to mobilize the military strength of the realm was made in 1588 to meet the approaching Spanish Armada. Walsingham, six months before the Armada came, asserted that he and Burghley between them had organized and trained 50,000 men for the defense of the kingdom and the Queen. These figures come close to a report two years later, which gave 42,000 trained men, 54,000 equipped but not trained, and 6,000 neither trained nor equipped.

If we estimate the trained bands at 50,000 men in the aggregate, we come as close to accuracy as the available figures support. It is worth noting, however, that of this array not more than 14,000 were mobilized when the Armada was actually in the Channel. This however does not include forces gathered in the North to guard the postern gate or in the maritime counties along the Channel to repel landings. One estimate puts the troops in the maritime counties at a little over 20,000.

Horsemen were furnished by the gentry in proportion to their means, by the clergy, and by the recusants. We have no complete figures of those forthcoming in 1588. Figures for the following year come to a little over 10,000.

Generally speaking, the trained bands were not used for military service outside England. For service in the Low Countries and in France troops were drafted, usually from the able-bodied unemployed, commonly known as rogues and vagabonds, or from the jails. William Lambarde pointed out that this accounted for the vagabond soldiers produced by the foreign wars. When they came back they had no jobs waiting for them; instead they joined the growing army of the unemployed and were a serious menace to peace because of the plundering habits developed in foreign service.

There was a good deal of corruption in the drafting of them by the local J.P's, who sometimes levied twice the number required and then allowed half of them to buy their way out. Sir John Falstaff made merry with the ragged regiments which were the fruits of this corruption. And yet the English soldier overseas turned out to be a good fighting man, even when he lacked pay and lacked food and went to battle in rags.

Shortly after Elizabeth ascended the throne she established a national church under royal supremacy. It was based upon the second Edwardian Prayer Book and on the Edwardian Articles of Faith, though with some conservative modifications. It was imposed upon the nation by an Act of Uniformity which provided severe punishment for those who administered or attended any other service. Those who refused to attend the established church were fined one shilling a Sunday and were subject to ecclesiastical censure. The fine was so small that it was not worth the expense of collecting it. Ecclesiastical censure might entail excommunication and unlimited imprisonment, though it rarely did. The choice was, indeed, between the established church and no church. Actually, the Act of Uniformity in its original form entailed very little physical hardship on the laity. And as for the clergy, though the Marian bishops with one exception refused to conform and were deprived, probably 95 per cent of the lower clergy accepted the new arrangements. Opposition to the Establishment came from the left and from the right—from the left by zealous Protestants who thought reform had not gone far enough; from the right from those who preferred the old faith. The radicals were a nuisance but not a menace; the Roman Catholics were at the start no more than passive resisters. We hear of them as recusants, refusers not rebels. In the remoter areas they often maintained old services and sheltered old priests. So long as they went no further the enforcement of the laws against them was languid. Without much doubt the old church steadily lost ground. There were no inquisitions, no martyrs, no stake. Elizabeth, as Francis Bacon observed, had no wish "to make windows into men's hearts and secret thoughts." So long as they behaved themselves, what they believed was their own affair. Her success, during the first decade of her reign, was the success of attrition, not of compulsion.

Later, when the Pope excommunicated the Queen, when missionaries from the Continent undertook to re-establish the old faith, and when discontented English Catholics supplied the background for numerous foreign plots against the Queen and the realm, the official attitude towards the recusants stiffened and the penalties for recusancy became crushingly heavy.

On the left, the radical Protestants, or Puritans as they came to be called, directed their efforts to the reform of the Establishment, attacking first the vestments of the clergy, then the ritual, ultimately the church government. They grew stronger as the reign progressed, not only among Englishmen at large but particularly among those in high places, in the House of Commons, even in Elizabeth's Privy Council. Many of them, through the instrumentality of the country gentry, found places in the church itself. Elizabeth was violently opposed to them because she regarded them as a dangerous menace, not only to her concept of church government but to the whole monarchial principle. But it was not until the last decade of her reign, when the defeat of the Spanish Armada had delivered her from the Roman Catholic menace, that she dealt vigorously with the Puritans. We hear little of them during the nineties. They had lost their old leaders and something of their old crusading zeal. They did not lose faith, but for the time being they stopped fighting.

The pattern of Anglican church government followed the Roman model. England was divided into two provinces, one with its headquarters at Canterbury, the other at York. Canterbury was much the larger, and the Archbishop of Canterbury was primate of England. He usually resided in London at

Lambeth Palace. The provinces were divided into dioceses under bishops, the dioceses into archdeaconries, and so down to the ultimate unit, the parish. The archbishop and bishops, though nominally elected, were actually appointed by the Crown. They were supported by what were called temporalities, that is to say, the revenues of lands held by the bishop in feudal tenure of the Queen. The income from temporalities varied. Durham, for example, and London, were much the richest sees in England. Others, like the Welsh bishoprics, were notoriously poor. Ambitious prelates always had their eyes on the rich sees, and sometimes spent more of their time promoting their interests at Court than was quite consistent with their ecclesiastical duties.

Elizabeth made systematic depredations upon episcopal temporalities. She not only kept offices vacant in order to enjoy the revenues, but she often drove hard bargains with new appointees. And she resorted to various other extortionate devices both for herself and her favorites. Sir Christopher Hatton and Sir Walter Raleigh both grew fat upon the ecclesiastical spoils.

What Elizabeth did at the top, the country gentry did at the bottom. In the parishes the rector was ordained by the bishop of the diocese, but was normally appointed by the lord of the manor who held the right of advowson, or by any other who had lawfully acquired the right either by purchase or by inheritance. Before the break from Rome the rector of the parish was normally supported by tithes, being one tenth of the annual produce of the soil. But in many cases the right to collect the tithes had passed, by way of the monasteries and the Crown, into the hands of lay impropriators, who assumed the obligation to supply religious services but generally managed to make a considerable profit out of the transaction. One way or another, either by the right of advowson or by impropriation of tithes, the parish clergy became creatures of the gentry, and that meant that the religious complexion of the parish often reflected the religious views of the lord of the manor or his equivalent. In the North he looked through his fingers at a scarcely disguised Roman Catholicism; in the South and East he often appointed a Puritan rector and nourished a Puritan congregation. It was one of these, in the next reign, that crossed the seas in the Mayflower and laid the foundations of New England.

The canon law of the medieval church and the ecclesiastical courts which administered it, except insofar as the papacy was concerned, survived the break from Rome and continued to have jurisdiction over those persons and in those cases which were recognized as its proper field.

It had jurisdiction, not only over all clergymen, but over those who could justify a claim to benefit of clergy. In the common law courts a man accused of felony could claim clergy and establish his claim by reading scripture, and so avoid capital punishment. Ben Jonson, the poet, escaped hanging by that appeal.

The church court also had jurisdiction over the laity in a variety of cases, such as marriage, kinship, testamentary inheritance, blasphemy, heresy, and other cases of the same sort. The line between what case belonged to the church courts and what to the courts of common law was an uncertain one and the cause of a good deal of dispute later.

So far as the average Englishman was concerned, his objection to the ecclesiastical courts was that they provided none of the safeguards for the defendant which he had come to regard as basic in English justice. There was no jury trial; the defendant could be forced to testify under oath against himself in matters incriminating. Legal or not, it was not British.

The chief offender in this regard was the so-called Court of High Commission, set up by the Queen in 1559 to implement the royal supremacy over the church. It was not primarily an ecclesiastical court but rather a prerogative court dealing particularly with offenses against the Acts of Supremacy and Uniformity. But it followed ecclesiastical procedure. In composition it was a mixed company of bishops, Privy Councillors, civilians, sergeants-at-law, and suchlike, nineteen all told in the original commission, of whom seven constituted a quorum. Later commissions enlarged the membership and reduced the number of the quorum, so that different sections could be sitting in different places at the same time. Archbishop Whitgift made use of it in his attack upon the Puritans and aroused a great deal of opposition among the friends of the Puritans in the House of Commons and the Privy Council. Lord Burghley wrote to Whitgift that though the canonists might defend it, it smacked too much of the Roman inquisition.

Whitgift stuck to his guns and with the help of the Queen rather more than held his own. But those who were arrayed against him, the Puritans and the common lawyers, carried on the fight and ultimately not only did away with the Court of High Commission but with the established church itself.

Elizabeth was not a reformer. She was innately a conservative, though a flexible one. No small part of her greatness lay in her ability to operate a government machine, already creaking in the joints, to the satisfaction of her people and the glory of her kingdom. What would happen when a less skilled hand was at the helm was a problem which she would not discuss or permit to be discussed.

# SUGGESTED READING

The best life of Elizabeth is by Sir John Neale, *Queen Elizabeth* (London, 1934; reprinted in a paperback, New York, 1957). Although it lacks footnotes, it is based throughout on sound scholarship. Sir John comes near to idealizing Elizabeth and needs to be tempered by J. A. Froude's estimate, which is definitely iconoclastic, in his *History of England from the Fall of Wolsey to the Death of Elizabeth* (12 vols., London, 1856–70), see Volumes 7–12, *The Reign of Elizabeth*.

On the constitutional history of the reign, Sir David Lindsay Keir's chapters in his *Constitutional History of Modern Britain, 1485–1937* (London, 1938), are as good as any; and there is a good deal of pertinent documentary material, with significant introductory notes, in Joseph R. Tanner, *Tudor Constitutional Documents, 1485–1603* (Cambridge, Eng., 1922, 1948). The chapters in Edward P. Cheyney, *A History of England from the Defeat of the Armada to the Death of Elizabeth* (2 vols., New York, 1914, 1926, 1948), particularly Part i in Volume I on the Royal Administration and Part viii in Volume II on Local Administration, are models of careful scholarship and clear exposition, though needing perhaps to be supplemented by Neale's admirable discussion of corruption in high places and exploitation of official positions for private profit in *The Elizabethan Political Scene* in *Proceedings of the British Academy*, Volume XXIV, 1948; also printed separately (London, 1948). The pertinent chapters in Wallace Notestein, *The English People on the Eve of Colonization, 1603–1630* (New York, 1954) are admirable, though they are more relevant to the reign of Elizabeth's successor, James I.

There is no adequate book on the Privy Council under Elizabeth. Its actual role can best be followed in the biographies of her two great secretaries, William Cecil and Francis Walsingham: Conyers Read, *Mr. Secretary Cecil and Queen Elizabeth* (London, 1955) and Mr. *Secretary Walsingham and the Policy of Queen Elizabeth* (3 vols., Oxford, 1925).

Sir John Neale's three volumes on Parliament under Elizabeth are as learned as they are interesting, and they displace all earlier works on the subject: *The Elizabethan House of Commons* (London, 1949), and *Elizabeth I and Her Parliaments* (2 vols., London, 1953–57), which has chiefly to do with the House of Commons and its relation to the crown. For the House of Lords, available source material is relatively scanty. Luke O. Pike, *Constitutional History of the House of Lords* (London, 1894) is useful but inadequate.

On public finance F. C. Dietz, *English Public Finance, 1558–1641* (New York, 1932) is the only adequate account, though it calls for corrections in detail.

For local government, Cheyney, cited above, is the best, though Notestein throws a good deal of light upon local officials such as the churchwardens and the constables. In this connection William Lambarde's *Eirenarcha* (London, 1581), the standard sixteenth-century handbook for justices, though hard to come by, is very helpful on matters of detail. Two MSS. by Lambarde in the Folger Library, one, *Ephemeris,* his diary as a justice of the peace in Kent, the other his addresses to the grand jury in Kent, are very illuminating. *Ephemeris* has been published (*Huntington Library Quarterly,* XV [1952], 123–58); the addresses to the grand jury are being prepared for the press.

Elizabethan courts of justice can be best pursued in Sir William Holdsworth's monumental *History of English Law* (12 vols., London, 1903–38). Prerogative courts have been subject to special study. For Chancery, Star Chamber, and Court of Requests, Cheyney gives the most succinct account. For the Court of Wards, two excellent books have recently appeared: H. E. Bell, *Introduction to the History and Records of the Court of Wards and Liveries* (Cambridge, Eng., 1953) and Joel Hurstfield, *The Queen's Wards* (London, 1958).

In matters ecclesiastical, the best narrative history of the Elizabethan church is Walter H. Frere, *History of the Church of England, 1558–1625* (London 1904). Felix Makower, *Constitutional History and Constitution of the Church of England* (Berlin, 1884; English trans., London, 1895) is still the standard, though difficult to use. John H. Pollen, as far as he goes (to 1581), is the best history of the Roman Catholics under Elizabeth: *The English Catholics in the Reign of Queen Elizabeth* (London, 1920). A. O. Meyer gives the complete story, best used in the English translation: *England and the Catholic Church under Elizabeth* (trans. by J. R. McKee, London, 1916, and revised by the author). There is nothing better than Knappen on English Puritanism: Marshall M. Knappen, *Tudor Puritanism* (Chicago, 1939).

John Strype's voluminous works, written early in the eighteenth century, particularly his *Annals of the Reformation* and his *Life and Acts of John Whitgift, D.D.* (Oxford, 1820–40, 1832), are gold mines of pertinent documents on Anglican church history, based largely on the Burghley papers in the Lansdowne MSS., British Museum, which were at one time in Strype's possession.

On the social philosophy supporting the structure of English society, the classical account is A. O. Lovejoy, *The Great Chain of Being* (Cambridge, Mass., 1936). As applied specifically to England it is well set forth by E. M. W. Tillyard in *The Elizabethan World Picture* (London, 1943).

For a more detailed bibliography on all of these subjects, see Conyers Read, *Bibliography of British History, Tudor Period* (Oxford, 1933; 2nd ed., Oxford, 1959).

*Plate 1.* Queen Elizabeth dressed as for the opening of Parliament. Engraved by Crispin van de Passe (1603–4) after a drawing by Isaac Oliver. From Humphrey Dyson, *A Book Containing All Such Proclamations As Were Published during the Reign of the Late Queen Elizabeth* (1618).

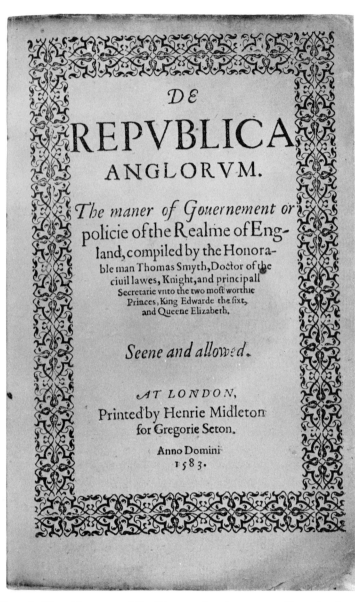

# DE
# REPVBLICA
## ANGLORVM.

*The maner of Gouernement or*
policie of the Realme of England, compiled by the Honora-
ble man Thomas Smyth, Doctor of the
ciuil lawes, Knight, and principall
Secretarie vnto the two most worthie
Princes, King Edwarde the sixt,
and Queene Elizabeth.

*Seene and allowed.*

*AT LONDON,*
Printed by Henrie Midleton
for Gregorie Seton.

Anno Domini
1583.

*Plate 2.* The title page of Sir Thomas Smith, *De republica Anglorum*
(1583).

30

*Plate 3.* The arms of England emblazoned by an anonymous artist. From Humphrey Dyson, *A Book Containing All Such Proclamations As Were Published during the Reign of the Late Queen Elizabeth* (1618).

*Plate 4.* Queen Elizabeth attended by three counselors. From a woodcut initial C in Gabriel Harvey, *Gratulationum valdinensium libri quatuor* (1578).

*Plate* 5. A proclamation against importing or possessing seditious books, March 1, 1568/69, printed for distribution the same date. The Queen's subjects are forbidden to have anything to do with books designed to corrupt their allegiance to the Queen and the established church, and are ordered to deliver up any such books in their possession to the bishop or other church official in their diocese within twenty-eight days after publication of the proclamation. Folger MS. X.d.85.

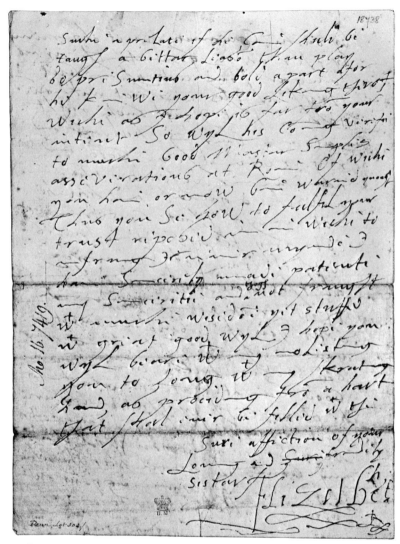

*Plate 6.* Part of a holograph letter of Elizabeth to James VI of Scotland, 5 January 1602/03. [BM Add. MS. 18738 f.39, courtesy of the British Museum.] The same letter is printed with variations in spelling from a copy in the library of Sir Peter Thompson in *Letters of Elizabeth and James VI*, ed. by John Bruce, Camden Society Publications, No. 46 (London, 1849.)

(The transcript below reproduces the spelling of the original except for the expansion of contractions such as wt and c̃ing.)

Suche a prelate if he come shuld be taugh a bettar leason than play so presumtius and bold a part afor he knewe your good liking therof wiche as I hope is far from your intent  So wyl his coming verefie to muche Good Mastar Simples asseverations at Rome òf wiche you haue or now bene warned ynough Thus you se how to fulfil your trust reposed in me wiche to infring I [ ] neuer mynde  I haue sincerely made patente my sinceritie and thogh not fraught with muche wisedome yet stuffed with great good wyl  I hope you wyl beare with my molesting you to long with my skrating hand, as prociding from a hart that shal euer be filled with the

sure affection of your
Louing and ~~sure~~ frindely
sistar

Elizabeth

R

*Plate 7.* William Cecil, first Baron Burghley, 1520–1598. Portrait by an unknown artist, courtesy of the National Portrait Gallery, London.

*Plate 8.* Robert Cecil, first Earl of Salisbury, 1563–1612. A portrait attributed to John De Critz, 1602, courtesy of the National Portrait Gallery, London.

*Plate 9.* Sir Francis Walsingham, 1536–1590. Portrait by an unknown artist, courtesy of the National Portrait Gallery, London.

In the image, text visible within the portrait:

LORD CHANCELLOR
HATTON 1589

TANDEM SI

*Plate 10.* Sir Christopher Hatton, 1540–1591. Portrait by an unknown artist, courtesy of the National Portrait Gallery, London.

*Plate 11*. Sir John Popham, 1531?–1607, Chief Justice and Speaker of the House of Commons. Portrait by an unknown artist, 1600, courtesy of the National Portrait Gallery, London.

*Plate 12.* Sir Nicholas Bacon, 1509–1579, Lord Keeper of the Great Seal. Portrait by an unknown artist, 1579, courtesy of the National Portrait Gallery.

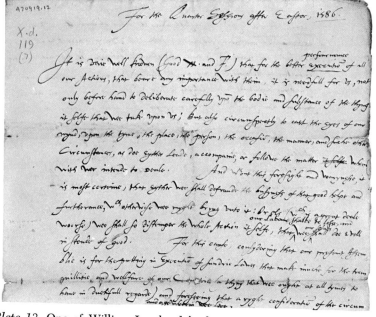

*Plate 13.* One of William Lambarde's charges to the jury as a justice of the peace in Kent: "For the Quarter Sessions after Easter, 1586." Folger MS. X.d.119 (7).

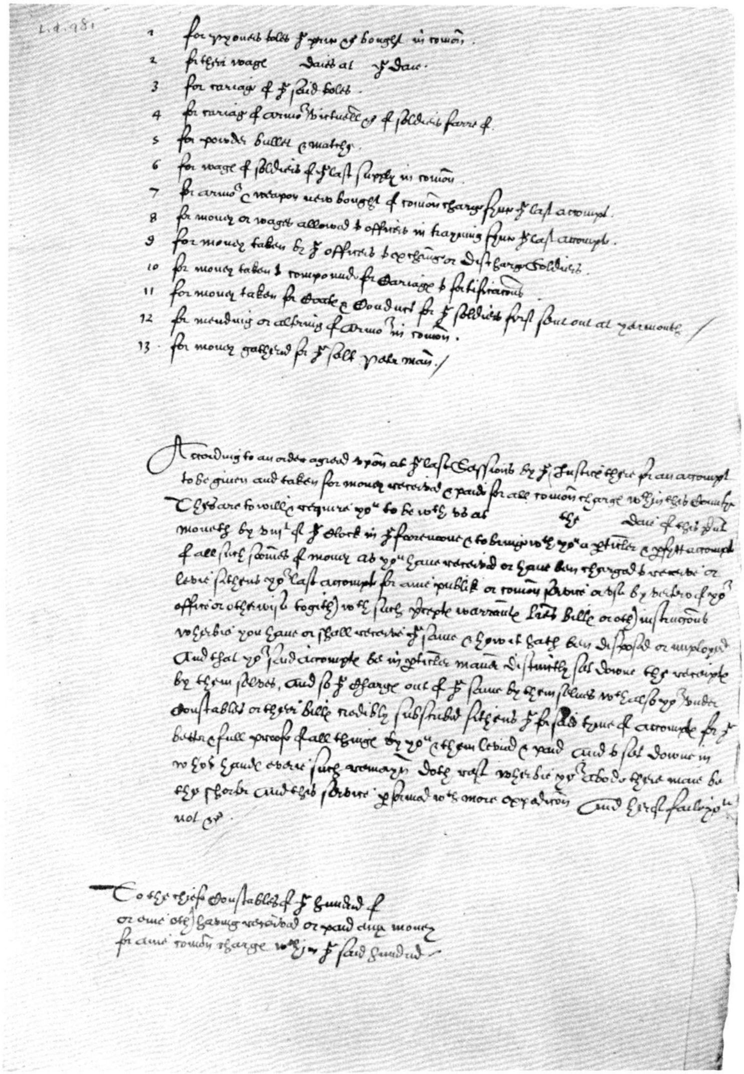

*Plate 14.* An order to the chief constables, probably of the county of Norfolk, regarding the rendering of accounts of expenses connected with their duties. From the Bacon-Townsend Papers, Folger MS. L.d.981.

43

*Plate 15.* The Queen opening a new Parliament in the White Chamber. From Robert Glover, *Nobilitas politica vel civilis* (1608).

*Plate 16.* The Parliament House, Westminster Hall, and Westminster Abbey engraved by Wenceslaus Hollar, 1647.

45

A VIEW of the COURT of WARDS and LIVERIES, with the *Officers, Servants*, and other *Persons* there assembled

*Plate 17.* Burghley presiding over a meeting of the Court of Wards and Liveries, engraved by George Vertue. The painting from which Vertue made his engraving was probably not the original but an early copy still in the collection of the Duke of Richmond. The portrait of the presiding master at the far end of the table closely resembles a miniature of Lord Burghley, with the same kind of hat, in the possession of the Marquess of Salisbury.

46